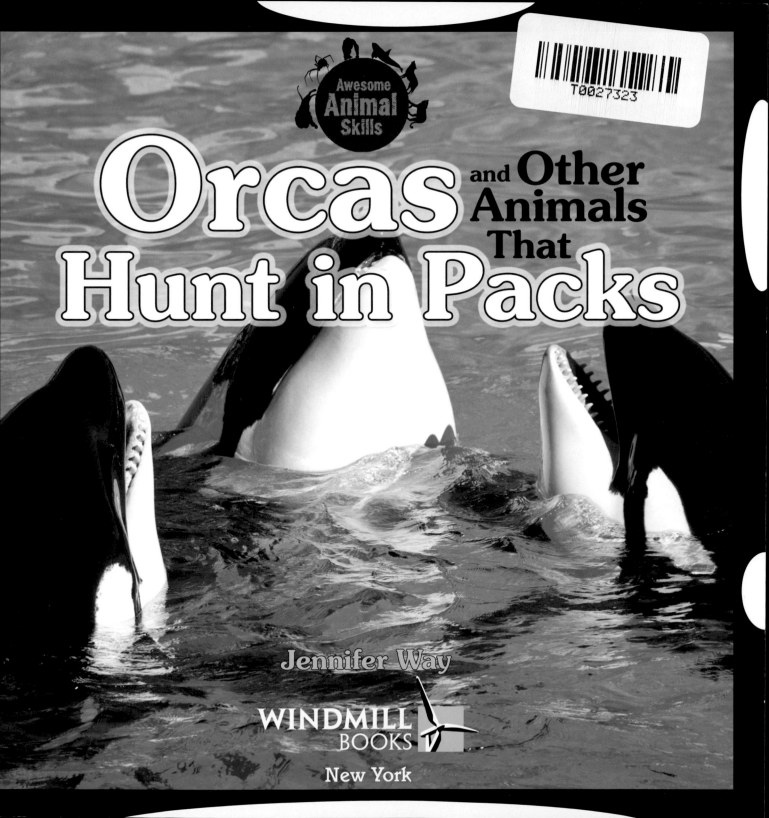

Awesome Animal Skills

Orcas and Other Animals That Hunt in Packs

Jennifer Way

WINDMILL BOOKS
New York

Published in 2016 by **Windmill Books**,
an Imprint of Rosen Publishing
29 East 21st Street, New York, NY 10010

Developed and produced for Rosen by BlueAppleWorks Inc.

Art Director: T.J. Choleva
Managing Editor for BlueAppleWorks: Melissa McClellan
Designer: Joshua Avramson
Photo Research: Jane Reid
Editor: Marcia Abramson

Photo Credits:
Cover left, p. 8 top left, FineShine/Shutterstock; cover right Catmando/Shutterstock; cover top riekephotos/Shutterstock; back cover, 24 top AnetaPics/Shutterstock; title page Chris Curtis/Shutterstock; TOC top SweetCrisis/Shutterstock; TOC bottom Twildlife/Dreamstime; p. 4 top left Dave Montreuil/Shutterstock; p. 4 top Daniel Padavona/Shutterstock; p.4 jurra8/Shutterstock; p. 5 top lenaer/Shutterstock; p. 5 bottom, 10 top Tory Kallman/Shutterstock; p. 6 top left Christian Musat/Shutterstock; p. 6 top Menno Schaefer/Shutterstock; p. 6 left Ivan Cholakov/Dreamstime; p. 6-7 Evgeniya Lazareva/Thinkstock; p. 8 top Karoline Cullen/Shutterstock; p. 8 Tomas Hajek/Dreamstime; p. 9 Kstokvis/Dreamstime; p. 9 top Sclowe/Dreamstime; p. 10 top left Mari Swanepoel/Shutterstock; p. 10 right Claude Huot/Shutterstock; p. 10 Claude Huot/Shutterstock; P. 11 Stephen Lew/Shutterstock; p. 12 top left Holly Kuchera/Thinkstock; p. 12 top kjekol/Thinkstock; p. 12 bottom John Pitcher/Thinkstock; p. 13 BMJ/Shutterstock; p. 12-13 Josef Pittner/Shutterstock; p. 14 top left guentermanaus/Shutterstock; p. 14 topachiaos/Shutterstock;p. 14 left Dennis Jacobsen/Dreamstime; p. 14-15 underworld/Shutterstock; p. 15 Dean Bertoncelj/Dreamstime; p. 16 top left Melissa Schalke/Dreamstime; p. 16 top Thomas Langlands/Dreamstime; p. 16 Shawn Jackson/Dreamstime; p. 17 atese/Thinkstock; p. 18 top left Mogens Trolle/Shutterstock; p. 18 top Michael Fitzsimmons/Thinkstock; p. 18 AndChisPhoto/Thinkstock; p. 18 right Dennis W. Donohue/Shutterstock; p. 19Peter Malsbury/Thinkstock; p. 19 righ AndreAnita/ Thinkstock; p. 20 top left Four Oaks/Shutterstock; p. 20 top Gualtiero Boffi/Dreamstime; p. 20 bottom Yatra/Shutterstock; p. 20-21 Claudio Beduschi/Thinkstock; p. 21 right Ecoimages/Shutterstock; p. 22 top left Atelopus/Thinkstock; p. 22 top Seanjeeves/Dreamstime;p. 22-23 Geoff Gallice/Creative Commons; p. 22 right, 23 bottom Dr. Morley Read/Shutterstock; p. 23 Karmesinkoenig/Creative Commons; p. 24 top left Michaelma198/Dreamstime; p 24 left EcoPrint/Shutterstock;p. 24-25 Hel080808/Dreamstime; p. 24 right ByronD/Thinkstock; p. 25 bottom Wolf Avni/Shutterstock;p. 26 top left apple2499/Shutterstock; p. 26 top Porojnicu Stelian/Shutterstock; p. 26 aaltair/Shutterstock; p. 27 kojihirano/Shutterstock; p. 27 right Tania Thomson/Shutterstock; p. 28 top leftPaul Wolf/Dreamstime; p. 28 top Achimdiver/Shutterstock; p. 28 middle Christin Khan, NOAA/Public Domain; p. 28-29 Evadb/Public Domain; p. 29 right Arturo de Frias Marques/Creative Commons.

Cataloging-in-Publication-Data

Way, Jennifer.
Orcas and other animals that hunt in packs / by Jennifer Way.
p. cm. — (Awesome animal skills)
Includes index.
ISBN 978-1-4777-5653-9 (pbk.)
ISBN 978-1-4777-5652-2 (6 pack)
ISBN 978-1-4777-5584-6 (library binding)
1. Killer whale — Juvenile literature. 2. Animal behavior — Juvenile literature.
3. Predatory animals — Juvenile literature. 3. Social behavior in animals — Juvenile literature.
I. Way, Jennifer. II. Title.
QL737.C432 W39 2016
599.53'6—d23

Manufactured in the United States of America
CPSIA Compliance Information: Batch #WS15WM: For Further Information contact: Rosen Publishing, New York, New York at 1-800-237-9932

CONTENTS

PREDATORS AND PREY

Animals that hunt other animals for food are called **predators**. A few examples of predators are orcas, wolves, and hyenas. Seals, deer, and wildebeests are examples of **prey** that these predators hunt. Predators use a variety of skills and hunting techniques to catch prey. Some hunt alone, others hunt in packs. Hunting in packs allows smaller predators to hunt much larger prey.

Peregrine falcons hunt alone. They rely on their swiftness as they swoop down at speeds of up to 200 miles per hour (322 km/h) to catch their prey.

PACK HUNTERS

Orcas use a technique called cooperative hunting, or hunting in packs. By hunting together using their communication skills, orcas have more success at catching prey than they would alone. Many animals that are cooperative hunters use communication and develop hunting **strategies**, while there are other pack hunters that work in less organized ways. No matter how they do it, pack hunters can take down more prey or bigger prey and hunt with less risk of injury than they can on their own. This book will show you how orcas earned their "killer whale" nickname and explore how other animals work together by hunting in packs.

Orcas hunt in packs. They are known to be able to work together to dislodge a seal from an iceberg.

DID YOU KNOW?

Orcas are known by a few different names. They are called killer whale, blackfish, and grampus. You are probably most familiar with the name killer whale. Scientists tend to avoid using this name because the orca is not actually a whale.

MYSTICAL ORCAS

Orcas are the largest members of the dolphin family. These **mammals** are generally between 23 and 32 feet (7 and 10 m) long and weigh up to 22,000 pounds (10,000 kg). Orcas are black on the top and the sides of their bodies and white on their underside. There is also a white patch on either side of the head. Orcas live in groups called pods. A pod can number up to 40 individuals. The group is made up of several generations of related orcas.

Mothers are the ones who raise the young and teach them how to hunt with the pod.

GREAT SWIMMERS

Orcas are found in all of the world's oceans, from the Arctic Ocean to the frigid waters of the Southern Ocean around Antarctica and to warmer waters near the equator. Orcas mostly prefer swimming in depths between 60 and 200 feet (18 and 61 m). They will also swim in shallow coastal waters or dive deep into the ocean in search of food. The pods **migrate** when prey becomes scarce.

Orcas live in three distinct types of social groupings. Resident orcas live in pods and migrate to the same places regularly. Transient orcas form small groups and do not form family bonds as strong as resident orcas. Offshore orcas travel far from the shore and gather in large groups to hunt schools of fish.

Orcas are highly social animals that travel in groups called pods. Orcas establish social orders, and pods are led by females.

TOP PREDATORS

The orca's large size and strength make it among the fastest marine mammals.

Orcas are **apex** predators. That means that they are the top predator in their **food chain** and have no predators. They are swift swimmers that can reach speeds of up to 35 miles per hour (56 km/h). Orcas have strong jaws with teeth that can be up to 4 inches (10 cm) long. The upper and lower teeth fit tightly together like a trap. This helps orcas keep a tight grip on prey.

Orcas do not chew their prey. Smaller animals, such as fish and small seals and sea lions, are swallowed whole. They eat larger animals, such as whales, by tearing off and swallowing large chunks. Orcas are big eaters that can consume 500 pounds (227 kg) of food per day!

TALKATIVE ORCAS

Orcas communicate with members of their pod using a wide variety of calls, clicks, and whistles. Each pod has its own dialect, or set of sounds, that is different from other pods' sounds. This dialect stays the same across generations of orcas! The pod members use their dialect to locate each other and to communicate with each other while they are hunting. Some of the animals orcas hunt include fish, sharks, sea turtles, seals, sea lions, and small whales and dolphins.

Orcas have keen senses of vision, touch, and hearing. This helps them find prey.

Because they are so smart, orcas are very good at catching marine mammals.

HUNTING TOGETHER

It is easiest for orcas to attack weak or young prey, but groups of five or more will go after healthy adults, even great white sharks! A hunt may take hours.

Orcas are sometimes called "wolves of the sea" because orca pods use cooperative hunting techniques similar to those of packs of wolves. An example of this is when a pod hunts a large animal, such as a blue whale. When an orca locates a whale, it will alert other members of the pod. The other pod members will then use that information to swim toward the prey. Next, the pod keeps communicating as they surround the whale and chase and attack it until the prey is dead.

Orcas also use echolocation to seek out prey. With **echolocation**, orcas emit high-pitched clicks that reflect off objects. When these sound waves bounce back, they tell orcas the location and other information about what is around them.

Often, to avoid injury, killer whales disable their prey before eating it. This may involve throwing it in the air.

DEADLY COOPERATION

Orcas also hunt fish together. When the pod finds a school of fish, the orcas will communicate so that they can herd the fish into a small area. This makes it easy for the orcas to scoop up and eat lots of fish. Orca pods also hunt animals resting on ice floes, such as penguins and seals. They slap their tails on the water to create waves that knock the prey off of the ice and toward waiting orcas' mouths!

11

CLEVER GRAY WOLVES

Gray wolves are the largest members of the dog family. An adult generally measures between 3 feet and 5 feet (0.9 and 1.5 m) from head to rear and weighs between 80 and 100 pounds (36 and 45 kg). Gray wolves once lived throughout much of the Northern Hemisphere, but today they are found in the northern part of North America, Europe, and Asia. They are **adaptable** to a variety of habitats, including forests, prairies, and tundra.

Wolves love pups. All the adults in a pack help to care for them, even though usually only the dominant pair are the actual parents.

DID YOU KNOW?

Domestic dogs are very closely related to the gray wolf. In fact, they are the same **species**. The domestic dog is a subspecies of the wolf. Tens of thousands of years of careful breeding has resulted in the tame behavior as well as the wide range of size and looks you see among today's dogs.

AFTER THE PREY

Wolves live in packs that typically have six to 12 members. The pack is made up of a **dominant** male, his **mate**, and their pups, and a few other adult wolves.

Hunting as a pack allows wolves to kill prey many times a wolf's size, such as bison, elk, moose, musk oxen, or reindeer. One wolf will use **vocalizations** to tell the rest of the pack when it sees prey to hunt. The wolves chase the prey until they have surrounded it and then they attack the prey together. After the prey is killed, these hunting machines become eating machines that can consume 20 pounds (9 kg) of meat in one sitting!

After working hard to bring down prey, the dominant male and female usually get to eat first.

BIG-TOOTHED PIRANHAS

Piranhas are freshwater fish that live in tropical rivers in South America. There are between 30 and 60 different species of piranha, and the red-bellied piranha is one of the most common. They are generally between 6 and 10 inches (15 and 25 cm) long, with flat greenish-brown bodies and red undersides. Piranhas have strong jaws with a single row of tightly packed blade-like teeth that can easily bite into animals.

Piranhas gather in a group called a shoal. The shoal is typically between 20 and 30 piranhas. It is a loose social structure that has two purposes. Its main purpose is to gain safety in numbers from predators such as caimans. The other purpose is for hunting.

STRONG IN NUMBERS

Piranhas hunt together in several ways. For example, the shoal will hide among the plants in the river and eat whatever animals swim by, such as insects, mollusks, and small fish. The shoal will also swim together to **scavenge** larger dead or weakened animals that are in the river.

DID YOU KNOW?

You might have heard about piranhas going into a "feeding frenzy" and eating a whole cow in a matter of minutes. This is largely a myth. Piranhas have only been known to do anything close to this when they have been penned together in large numbers and starved before having a dead animal tossed into the water.

Most piranhas eat insects, worms, fish, crustaceans, and scavenged scraps, but not all. At least one species is vegetarian.

BRAINY DOLPHINS

Dolphins belong to the same family as orcas. Dolphins live in groups called pods, which can number from just a few dolphins to dozens of members. As do orcas, dolphins communicate using sounds such as whistles and clicks, and seek prey using echolocation. One of the most common dolphins is the bottlenose dolphin. These sleek, gray mammals are generally between 10 and 14 feet (3 and 4.3 m) long and weigh around 1,000 pounds (454 kg). Bottlenose dolphins are found in tropical, subtropical, and in warmer **temperate** ocean water all around the world.

Bottlenose dolphins love to play, though they are not really smiling when they do. Their mouths are shaped into a permanent curve.

Dolphins help sick or injured members of their pod. They surround the hurt dolphin to protect it from predators such as sharks. They also help the dolphin get to the surface to breathe air.

In order to capture the most prey, dolphins work in teams. Bottlenose dolphins mainly eat fish, but also squid and shrimp.

SHARING THE CATCH

Dolphins are intelligent hunters who use two cooperative hunting techniques called herding and corralling. Herding is when dolphins surround a group of fish, shrimp, or squid and force them to stay in a small area. Then each dolphin takes a turn grabbing the prey in their sharp teeth and swallowing it whole. Corralling is when the dolphins chase prey into shallow water, so that the prey is trapped between the dolphins and the shore. Once again, the dolphins take turns eating the prey.

MAGNIFICENT LIONS

> Each lion pride consists of one to three adult males, up to a dozen females, and their cubs. The females usually are all related to each other.

Lions are members of the cat family. These "big cats" are usually between 4.5 and 6.5 feet (1.4 and 2 m) long and weigh between 260 and 425 pounds (118 and 193 kg). Lions live in a warm, dry, grassy habitat called **savanna**. The most common lions are African lions, which live in Africa south of the Sahara Desert. Asiatic lions are a smaller population of lions that live in India's Gir Forest.

PRIDE ON A HUNT

Lions live in family groups called prides. The females are the main hunters for the pride, while the male lions stay behind to watch the cubs.

When lions hunt, they stalk and **ambush** their prey. They prefer large animals such as zebras, wildebeests, impalas, and gazelles. They will look for an individual that is slower or weaker than the rest of its herd. Then they surround the prey, sneaking closer and relying on their fur to camouflage them among the bushes and grass. Next, the lions spring forth, chasing the prey to the center of the hunting group. Finally, the strongest lion leaps onto the prey and kills it by strangling it in its jaws.

Female lions team up to form hunting parties. Working together, they are not afraid to attack animals much larger than a single lioness.

TIRELESS HYENAS

There are three species of hyena: spotted hyenas, brown hyenas, and striped hyenas. Spotted hyenas are the largest of the species. They all have large heads, long necks, and longer front legs than rear legs. They live in savannas and scrubby woodlands in Africa, Asia, and the Middle East. Hyenas live in groups called clans, which can have from three up to 80 members. The clan is led by a dominant female. Females stay with the clan they are born into, but males must find their place in another clan once they become an adult.

Hyenas crunch bones with their strong jaws. Their stomachs can digest bone and skin.

CLAN CHASE

Hyenas communicate using a variety of vocal sounds, such as whoops, grunts, growls, and a laughing sound. These sounds serve as greetings, and tell clan members where others are, or if the clan has killed prey.

Hyenas are swift hunters, able to chase prey without tiring. They hunt mostly herd animals, such as gazelles, zebras, and wildebeests. The larger the clan, the larger the prey they can take down. The clan works together to separate a slow or sick animal from its herd. Then they chase it until it collapses. The clan then scrambles to eat the prey based on their standing within the group.

Hyenas often must defend their food from other animals. They work in teams to do this.

Army ants live in tropical forests in Central America and South America. They live in colonies, a group that can have 100,000 to 2,000,000 members! Colonies are headed by queens, who lay all of the colonies' eggs. Worker ants are non-queen females, and are the members who care for the eggs, build the nest, and leave to hunt for food.

Like a human army at war, these ants keep moving, and that is how they got their name. They need to travel in order to find enough prey to feed everyone, so they build only temporary nests. The workers cooperate to kill and carry prey back to the nest. They hunt mostly other insects, such as wasps, crickets, and cockroaches, as well as spiders and scorpions. The ants swarm the prey, overtaking it with painful stings. They use their powerful mandibles, or jaws, to pull off legs, antennae, and other parts to carry back to the nest.

Army ants need lots of prey to feed their young. A queen can produce millions of eggs a month.

Like other ants, army ants communicate with the members of their colony using chemicals made by their body, which they can smell.

When the army marches, worker ants kill all the other insects, spiders, and even reptiles in their path. The colony can eat up to 500,000 prey each day.

Large soldier ants defend the colony and have giant mandibles. Smaller worker ants gather prey or care for immature ants as they march.

23

CAUTIOUS MEERKATS

Meerkats live in the deserts and open savannas of southern Africa. These small mammals are roughly the size of a squirrel. They are often seen standing on their hind legs near their **burrows**, carefully keeping watch for predators.

Meerkats live in groups called mobs. A mob can have up to 30 members, consisting of up to three families. Fathers and older siblings help the mothers raise and protect the younger pups. All of the adult meerkats teach the young how to hunt and how to stay alert to danger.

Guards watch for hawks, eagles, snakes, and jackals that hunt meerkats. The whole mob takes cover if they hear a warning call.

LOOKOUTS

When meerkats are hunting, at least one member of the mob stands guard. The guard is keeping a lookout for predators that prey on meerkats, such as hawks. Meerkats' eyes are adapted to help them spot predators. They have wide-angle vision. They also have black bands around their eyes that reduce glare from the sun. When a guard sees danger, it calls out to the mob to hide. The meerkats rotate guarding duty, making a vocalization to mark that it is time to switch. They take turns guarding so that every member gets a chance to hunt for insects, spiders, and other small animals.

Meerkats do not store fat in their lean bodies, so they must eat every day. They forage together but dine alone.

SHREWD PELICANS

American white pelicans nest together in colonies of as many as 5,000 pairs. Both parents guard eggs and raise chicks.

Pelicans are easily recognizable by the throat pouch, which they use to catch fish. There about a half dozen species of these birds living in warm and temperate coastal areas and areas near lakes and rivers around the world. Pelicans travel in flocks of dozens of members. The flock makes a yearly migration from their home area for mating season. Pelicans choose a partner for the mating season, and they build a nest, which they guard against other pelicans in the mating colony.

Brown pelicans are smaller than American white pelicans. They also hunt differently. They dive headfirst into the water to snatch up prey that they spot from the air.

TEAM EFFORT

The American white pelican is an example of a species that hunts in groups. They like to come together in groups of a dozen or more birds to feed, as they can thus cooperate and corral fish to one another. A flock will swoop low and flap their wings on the surface of the water. They will do this while flying in a U formation that is moving toward the land. These actions drive fish into shallow water, where the pelicans can scoop them up into their pouch. The pelicans then tilt their head to drain out the water from the pouch and swallow the fish whole.

CUNNING HUMPBACK WHALES

Humpback whales live near ocean coastlines, migrating from cool polar waters in the summer to warmer tropical waters in the winter. Humpbacks are typically between 50 and 60 feet (15 and 18 m) long and weigh as much as 80,000 pounds (36,000 kg).

Humpback whales travel in loosely organized pods. Mothers and their young swim close together, often touching one another with their flippers. Humpbacks communicate with other pod members through "songs" made up of a series of howls, cries, and other noises.

Whale songs travel far through the seas. Scientists are trying to learn their exact meanings.

LUNCH FOR CHAMPIONS

Although humpback whales are huge, they eat small animals, such as krill, plankton, and small fish. Humpbacks have several hunting techniques, but "bubble fishing" is the one done cooperatively by the pod. The whales blow bubbles while swimming in a circle under the water. The bubbles have a netlike effect on the prey, forcing them into a small area. Then the whales swim into that area and pull the prey into their mouths. They close their mouths and push the water back out through their baleen plates. Baleen plates act like filters to let the water out but keep the prey in the whale's mouth. Humpback whales need to eat between 4,000 and 5,000 pounds (1,814 and 2,268 kg) of food per day!

When humpback whales bubble fish, they force hundreds of prey to the surface of the ocean. Seagulls and other birds flock to take advantage of the easy fishing.

GLOSSARY

ADAPTABLE Able to change or be changed in order to work better.

AMBUSH To attack by surprise from a hidden place.

APEX The top.

BURROWS Holes or tunnels in the ground that animals live in.

DOMINANT More powerful than others in a group.

ECHOLOCATION A process for locating distant or invisible objects by means of sound waves reflected back to the sender from the objects.

FOOD CHAIN A series of types of living things in which each one uses the next lower member of the series as a source of food.

MAMMALS Warm-blooded vertebrates that nourish their young with milk and have skin covered with hair.

MATE A partner for making babies.

MIGRATE To pass from one region to another usually on a regular schedule for feeding or breeding.

PREDATORS Animals that eat other animals for food.

PREY Animals that are eaten by other animals.

SAVANNA A grassland containing scattered trees.

SCAVENGE To collect edible things from what has been left behind.

SPECIES A group of living things of the same kind and with the same name. All people are one species.

STRATEGIES Careful plans or methods.

TEMPERATE A climate that is usually mild without extremely cold or extremely hot temperatures.

VOCALIZATIONS Acts, processes, or instances of making sounds with the mouth and vocal cords.

FOR MORE INFORMATION

Further Reading

Marsh, Laura. *Meerkats*.
Des Moines, IA: National Geographic Children's Books, 2013.

Meinking, Mary. *Lion vs. Gazelle*.
North Mankato, MN: Raintree Books, 2011.

Simon, Charman, and Ariel Kazunas. *Killer Whales*.
New York, NY: Scholastic, 2012.

Simon, Seymour. *Dolphins*.
New York, NY: Harper Collins, Reprint edition, 2011.

WEBSITES

For web resources related to the subject of this book, go to:
www.windmillbooks.com/weblinks and select this book's title.

INDEX